THE LITTLE WITCH PRESENTS

A MONSTER JOKE BOOK

THE LITTLE WITCH PRESENTS

A

MONSTER JOKE BOOK

by
Linda Glovach and Charles Keller

Prentice-Hall, Inc., Englewood Cliffs, New Jersey

Printed in the United States of America   •J

Prentice-Hall International, Inc., London
Prentice-Hall of Australia, Pty. Ltd., North Sydney
Prentice-Hall of Canada, Ltd., Toronto
Prentice-Hall of India Private Ltd., New Delhi
Prentice-Hall of Japan, Inc., Tokyo
Prentice-Hall of Southeast Asia Pte. Ltd., Singapore

10 9 8 7 6 5 4 3 2 1

Library of Congress Cataloging in Publication Data
Glovach, Linda.
    The little witch presents a monster joke book.

    SUMMARY: The Little Witch presents a collection of
jokes, riddles, and rhymes featuring ghosts, vampires,
skeletons, and monsters of various sorts.
    1. Wit and humor, Juvenile. [1. Joke books]
I. Keller, Charles, joint author. II. Title.
PZ8.7.G5Li   [817]   76-9077
ISBN 0-13-537993-8

For Coby, Bayard, Paul and Jackie
C.K.

To Uncle Pat
L.G.

THE LITTLE WITCH PRESENTS

A MONSTER JOKE BOOK

Is it bad luck if a black cat follows you?
· *That depends on whether you're a man or a mouse.*

What did the hippy say to the invisible man?
· *"Man, you're out of sight."*

What do ghosts ride on in the amusement park?
· *The roller ghoster.*

What did the old witch say to the twin witches?
· *"Which witch is which?"*

What did the ghost say when he walked into the liquor store?

• *"Do you serve spirits here?"*

A skeleton in a carton
Invited a ghost to his room.
They spent the whole night
In the eeriest fight
About who should be frightened of whom.

Boy: There was a monster in my house last night.
Girl: How do you know?
Boy: I saw his motorcycle parked outside. I think
he was walking around in the refrigerator.
Girl: How can you be sure?
Boy: I saw his footprints in the jello.

Monster: Did you hear about Freddy? He died
when he drank a gallon of varnish.
Second monster: That's too bad.
Monster: Yes, but they say he had a lovely finish.

There was a monster from Mars
Who liked to eat under the stars.
He ate things of wood
Because they were good
And left his mouth all full of scars.

Why doesn't the devil ice skate?
· *Where in hell would he find ice?*

Ghost: May I haunt your house?
Man: Sure, be my ghost.

What happened when the monster swallowed uranium?

· *It got atomic ache.*

In the dark, dark world
There's a dark, dark country;
In the dark, dark country
There are dark, dark woods;
In the dark, dark woods
There's a dark, dark house;
And in the dark, dark house
There's a man trying to fix a fuse.

What would you do if the Frankenstein monster and Count Dracula were at your door?

· *Hope it was Halloween.*

Where does a ten foot monster sleep?
· *Anywhere it wants.*

What did the witch's broom say to her baby?
· *"Go to sweep little baby."*

Why did dragons sleep during the daytime?
· *So they could hunt knights.*

When do witches cook eggs?
· *On Fry Day.*

What did the skeleton say in the cold weather?
· *"The wind goes right through me."*

How does Dracula make a jail?
· *With blood cells.*

Where are monsters found?
· *Monsters are so big they never get lost.*

What has two legs, two arms, and two heads?
· *A two-headed monster.*

What did the monster say when it fell in love with the gorilla?
· *"Gorilla my dreams, I love you."*

Why did the farmer have a hair-raising experience?

· *Because he owned a rabbit farm.*

What did the monster say to the gas pump?

· *"Take your finger out of your ear and listen to me."*

Why did the witch take the airplane to New York?

· *Her broom was in the repair shop.*

What did one witch say to the other when they went fishing?
· *"Shall we cast a spell?"*

How do you get a broom to fly?
· *Buy it an airplane ticket.*

Why didn't the monster go to college?
· *His extension cord was too short.*

What do werewolfs sing when they go to a party?
· *"Howl, howl, the gang's all hair."*

Where do ghosts mail their letters?
· *At the ghost office.*

What's the ghost capital of the United States?
· *Casper, Wyoming.*

Ghost: I hear you have a new ghoul friend.
Vampire: Yes, it was love at first fright.
Ghost: It's no wonder. She's so boo-tiful.

What do you get if you cross a vampire with a skunk?

· *A dirty look from the vampire.*

In the days of King Arthur, a knight
Was bragging of how he could fight.
But while he was braggin'
There entered a dragon
That put him in unknightly flight.

What do they call the land where monsters live?

· *A terrortory.*

What's yellow and very dangerous?
· *Shark-infested applesauce.*

What did the monster say when it sat on a box of cookies?
· *"That's the way the cookie crumbles."*

What's green, noisy and very dangerous?
· *A herd of stampeding pickles.*

What did the monster say when the Volkswagen
ran into him?
· *How many times have I told you kids not to play
in the street?*

What did the one witch say to the other when she
tried to hitch a ride?
· *"There's always broom for one more."*

Why did silly Billy think the school was haunted?
· *Because the teacher told him about the school
spirit.*

How do monsters earn extra money?
· *By babysitting for witches on Saturday nights.*

What do vampires say when they play cops and robbers?
· *"Fang, fang, you're dead."*

What did the coach say to the ghost when he scored a touchdown?
· *"That's the spirit."*

Why doesn't lightning strike twice in the same place?
· *It doesn't have to. After the first time the place isn't there anymore.*

Where are the best T.V. horror shows seen?
· *On a ghost to ghost network.*

What do you call a skeleton that pushes your doorbell?
· *A dead ringer.*

Why did Dracula hang upside down in the phone booth?
· *Because he couldn't hang up.*

To what family does the werewolf belong?
· *I don't know. Nobody on our block has one.*

What prize did the witch's broom win?
· *The sweepstakes.*

Knock, knock.
Who's there?
Boo.
Boo who?
What are you crying for?

What is a ghost's favorite pie?
· *Boo-meringue.*

What do witches eat at the beach?
· *Sand-witches.*

What did the boy say to the ghost?
· *Nothing. He just ran.*

Where can you buy a monster?
· *At a monster sale.*

What does a hundred pound mouse say to the witch's black cat?
· *"Here, kitty, kitty."*

What goes clomp, swish — clomp, swish — clomp, swish?
· *A monster with a wet tennis sneaker.*

What's huge and has purple feet?
· *A monster that makes his own wine.*

What do you get when you cross a monster with a greyhound?
· *A monster that seats forty-five people.*

Vampire: Do you know any good jokes?
Ghoul: What kind of jokes do you like?
Vampire: Something in a light vein.

Boy: I'm stronger than King Kong.
Girl: How do you know?
Boy: I can beat my chest without hollering.

What kind of diapers does a baby ghost wear?
· *Vampers.*

How do you get a vampire out of a tub of jello?
· *Follow the directions on the box.*

What do you get when you cross a ten-foot
monster with a computer?
· *A ten-foot know-it-all.*

What does a vampire do first thing at night?
· *He puts on his bat-robe and brushes his teeth in
the bat-room.*

Boy: What does your father do?
Girl: He's a magician. He saws women in half.
Boy: Do you have any brothers?
Girl: No, but I have three half-sisters.

Girl: I spoke to a two-headed monster yesterday.
Boy: What did he say?
Girl: Hello, hello. How are you? How are you?

How does a ghost eat an apple?
· *By gobblin it.*

What monster ruled the waves?
· *The British Vampire.*

Why do vampires live in coffins?
· *Because the rent is low.*

Vampire: A panhandler came up to me yesterday
and told me he hadn't had a bite in days.
Second vampire: What did you do?
Vampire: I bit him.

Ghost: What's your favorite tourist spot?
Vampire: The Vampire State Building. But people don't like me to go there.
Ghost: Why?
Vampire: They say I'm a pain in the neck.

Girl: What are you doing?
Boy: Whistling to keep the ghosts away.
Girl: But there aren't any ghosts around here.
Boy: See? It's working.

Boy: Why do you witches always ride brooms?
Witch: Because vacuum cleaners are too heavy.

What is the best way to talk to a monster?
· *Long distance.*

Man: What happened to that saw-a-woman-in-half act you used to do?
Magician: My assistant left me. She moved to New York and Los Angeles.

Why did ten monsters walk down the street
dressed in blue shirts?

· *They were all on the same softball team.*

First mummy: I tried to get you on the phone
yesterday.
Second mummy: I couldn't answer; I was all tied
up. Why did you call me?
First mummy: I thought we could have a wrap
session.

What does a monster do when he breaks a toe?

· *Gives up ballet.*

Scientist: I just crossed a vampire and a mummy.
Reporter: What did you get?
Scientist: I'm not sure. It's either a flying band-aid
or a gift-wrapped bat. I don't know what to call it,
but I'm sure it will always get a seat on the bus.

Sitting on a tombstone,
A ghost came up and said,
"Sorry to disturb you,
But you're sitting on my head."

Baby: Mommy, what's a vampire?
Mother: Don't ask silly questions. Drink your
tomato juice before it clots.

What kind of car does a vampire drive?
· *A bloodmobile.*

Doctor: You look terrible. You're white as a sheet.
Ghost: I know. I feel terrible. Someone mixed me
in with the bedclothes when they did the laundry.

What do monsters eat?
· *Canned monster food.*

Where do monsters come from?
· *Great big storks.*

First ghost: How much do you charge to haunt a house?

Second ghost: That depends on how many rooms it has. Did you ever haunt one?

First ghost: No, I don't have a haunting license.

How do you know if a vampire has a cold?
· *By his coffin.*

What do they do with old bowling balls?
· *They give them to monsters to shoot marbles with.*

Ghost: Did you go to the dance last night?
Skeleton: Yes, but I had no body to dance with.
Ghost: Did you leave?
Skeleton: No, I didn't have the guts.

What are a baby monster's parents called?
· *Dead and mummy.*

Ghost: I hear you got a new boat.
Vampire: Yes, it's a blood vessel.
Ghost: Where do you sail it?
Vampire: On the Eerie Canal.

Can you escape from a monster by carrying a
blazing torch?

· *Yes, if you carry the torch fast enough.*

What did the mad scientist see in his frying pan?
· *An unidentified frying object.*

What's green and can walk through walls?
· *Casper, the friendly pickle.*

What color is a ghost?
· *Boo.*

What's six feet long and has eight eyes?
· *A monster's sneakers.*

What is the scientific name for a shrunken head?
· *A dehydrated noodle.*

Why did the ghost sleep on the roof of the house?
· *To keep up his spirits.*

Boy: I saw a horror movie on TV last night.
Girl: What was it about?
Boy: Boy meets girl, boy loses girl, boy creates new girl.
Girl: It sounds like it was written by a ghost writer.

What's red, white, and blue and scares people?
• *A patriotic monster.*

Who started the monster jokes?
• *That's what the monsters want to know.*